T0063178

# The Life, Teaching, and Legacy of
## *Martin Luther*

ANDREW J. LINDSEY

WESTBOW
PRESS
A DIVISION OF THOMAS NELSON

Unless otherwise noted, all Scripture passages are the author's translation.

WestBow Press books may be ordered through booksellers or by contacting:

WestBow Press
A Division of Thomas Nelson
1663 Liberty Drive
Bloomington, IN 47403
www.westbowpress.com
1 (866) 928-1240

ISBN: 978-1-4908-1996-9 (sc)
ISBN: 978-1-4908-1998-3 (hc)
ISBN: 978-1-4908-1997-6 (e)

Library of Congress Control Number: 2013922866

Printed in the United States of America.

WestBow Press rev. date: 12/17/2013

# Contents

Introduction ............................................................. ix

1. Origin, Education, and the Monastery ..............1

2. Early Monastic Career, First Mass, and
the Pilgrimage to Rome ...................................... 7

3. Professorship in Wittenberg and
Evangelical Experience ......................................15

4. Background to the 95 Theses...........................21

5. Posting the 95 Theses .....................................31

6. Interview With Cardinal Cajetan .................... 37

7. The Leipzig Disputation and the Papal Bull .... 45

8. The Diet of Worms............................................ 53

9. "Sir George" ..................................................... 65

10. Marriage and Family Life .................................71

11. The Augsburg Confession ............................... 79

12. Death and Legacy ............................................ 83

Endnotes ................................................................ 93

Bibliography............................................................ 99

Dedicated to Dr. Shawn D. Wright,
Associate Professor of Church History,
The Southern Baptist Theological Seminary,
who helped re-ignite my interest in Martin Luther
and appreciate his relevance for today.

Thanks to my wife (Abby Lindsey) and
to my mother (Theresa Lindsey)
for invaluable help in editing this work.

## Romans 1:17

For in [the gospel] the righteousness of God is revealed from faith unto faith, just as it has been written, "The just man by faith will live."

It is my goal in writing this work to render an account of Martin Luther's life that is brief, simple, accurate, and evangelical.

In twelve short chapters, I give a brief sketch of Luther's life, touching upon major events in his life, major controversies in which he was involved, major works that he published, and major doctrines that he taught. I hope to give readers a firm basis for doing further research into the life of this great reformer.

I have endeavored to make this work accessible even for readers who may still be in middle school or underclassmen in high school. (I began writing this book as I was teaching about the life of Martin Luther to fifth and sixth graders at Sayers Classical Academy in Louisville, Kentucky.) I have tried to keep the language simple, and when more complicated terms were necessary— such as "justification," "purgatory," "indulgences," "merits," or even "supererogation"— I have either directly defined the terms in the text or have tried to write in such a way that readers may gain a sense of these terms' definitions from the immediate contexts in which they occur.

In seeking to compose a compelling biography, I have striven to relate the events of Martin Luthers' life with a strict attention to historical accuracy. Martin Luther was a folk hero in his own day, and many legends sprang up concerning his various activities. Some previous simple, introductory biographies of Martin Luther have suffered from uncritically repeating these legends. Untruths are particularly out of place, however, in writing about someone who devoted his life to proclaiming the truth of the gospel.

As I was discussing the life of Martin Luther with my fifth and sixth grade classes at Sayers Classical Academy in Louisville, I was dismayed to find that my students had— from the particular biography that they were then reading, which will go unnamed here— gained no real sense concerning the occasion on which Martin Luther was converted to true faith in Christ. Indeed, the students seemed to think that Martin Luther was born again when he cried out to St. Anne and then became a monk! Martin Luther's crisis of faith, his failed attempts to resolve this crisis through taking monastic vows, and the resolution that he eventually found to this crisis in prayerfully meditating on the words from Romans 1:17— "The just shall live by faith"— may be difficult for young readers to grasp, but it is crucial for a person to think on these issues if he or she is to understand Luther's life story and Luther's insight into the good news concerning the life, death, burial, and resurrection of the Lord Jesus Christ on behalf of sinners.

It is my sincere hope that readers find this short biography of Martin Luther to be informative, interesting, and spiritually edifying.

-Andrew J. Lindsey: Louisville, KY; March 4, 2013.

# Chapter 1

# Origin, Education, and the Monastery

Martin Luther was born on November 10, 1483 in Eisleben, Germany to Hans and Margaret Luther (originally the family name was Luder; this was later changed). Hans and Margaret probably named their son Martin because November 10 was known as Saint Martin's Eve. In time, Hans and Margaret Luther had several other children: both boys and girls.[1]

Hans Luther was of peasant heritage, and his work history shows how peasants in the late Middle Ages could improve their place in society. He became a middle-class silver miner and then an owner of several foundries. Hans expected his eldest son to continue improving the Luther family fortune; he was to be given the best education possible and seek a job that would increase his family's wealth.[2]

Martin Luther's childhood was not a happy one. His parents were extremely strict. In the late Middle Ages, children were generally treated much more severely than they are today. But even by those standards, Luther seems to have endured an especially hard time. As an adult, Luther would still speak bitterly of the punishments he had suffered as a child.[3]

Martin Luther's first experience of discipline at school was no better than the punishments he received at home. He later spoke of having been brutally whipped for not perfectly memorizing his difficult lessons. His grammar school education took place in Mansfeld, Germany. In 1497-98, Luther attended a school run by the Franciscan Brothers (an order of monks) at Magdeburg, Germany. As was typical at that time, the school required Luther and other students to go into the town and beg for daily food. From 1498 to 1501 Luther went to school in Eisenach, Germany, where he lived with and was cared for by the Cotta family.[4]

In 1505, at the age of twenty-one, Martin Luther earned his Master of Arts degree at Erfurt, Germany. He then planned to enter law school, as his father wanted him to become a lawyer. However, Martin Luther had become extremely concerned about the condition of his soul: whether he would be accepted or condemned before God on the Day of Judgment. In Martin Luther's view, the path that offered the greatest possible hope of salvation was complete dedication to spiritual matters by becoming a monk. Luther knew that such a decision would enrage his father. The family's financial security and increased social standing was pinned on the hope of Martin Luther becoming a successful lawyer.[5]

In July of 1505, Martin Luther was returning to school in Erfurt after a visit with his parents. A sudden thunderstorm arose, and Luther was caught out in the pouring rain. Lightning struck the ground a short distance away from Luther, knocking him down. He feared that he was about to die! In terror, Martin called out to St. Anne: his father's favorite saint. (She was thought to be the mother of the Virgin Mary and was the patron saint of miners.) "St. Anne! Help me! I will become a monk!" His vow to St. Anne—made in a moment of terror—was to shape the course of Luther's life. After safely returning to Erfurt, Luther was determined to keep his promise. That month, without his father's knowledge (and against his father's wishes) Martin Luther joined the Augustinian monastery in Erfurt.[6]

**Focus Verse**: "I, even I, am the LORD, and except for me there is no savior" (Isaiah 43:11).

## Questions for Reflection and Discussion

1. Why did Martin Luther first consider becoming a monk, and what kept him from immediately joining the monastery?

2. To whom did Martin Luther call out when he feared for his life in the lightning storm?

3. Think of a difficult or frightening situation you have faced. What was your first response?

Martin Luther in the Lightning Storm

# Chapter 2

## Early Monastic Career, First Mass, and the Pilgrimage to Rome

During his first year in the monastery, Martin Luther was designated as a novice. During this time, called the novitiate, the other monks determined whether the novice was sincere in his desire to become a monk.[7] The days of a novice were filled with religious exercises designed to bring his soul into a state of peace before God.[8] Prayers were conducted at seven specific times each day. In between prayer times, the monk was engaged in chores or studies at the monastery, or he begged for food in the neighboring town.

Because Martin Luther was plagued by doubts about whether his monastic endeavors were truly freeing him from his sin, he began to engage in even more severe practices than those undertaken by the other monks. Luther would fast: sometimes three days in a row without a crumb. He would also refuse any blankets while sleeping in the cold. He nearly froze to death![9] Luther later testified:

> *I was a good monk, and I kept the rule of my order so strictly that I may say that if ever a monk got to heaven by his monkery*

> *it was I. All my brothers in the monastery who knew me will bear me out. If I had kept on any longer, I would have killed myself with vigils, prayers, readings, and other work.*[10]

As Martin was enduring hardship in the monastery, the Luther family was enduring hardships of their own. Only a few months after Martin Luther had angered his father by entering the monastery, the plague swept through Mansfeld. Two of Luther's brothers died. Hans Luther's heart was nearly broken. Then someone came to Mansfeld to report that Martin, a monk in the Erfurt monastery, was also dead. When Hans finally learned that it was another Martin, and not his son, who had died, the father vowed to have a more forgiving attitude.[11]

When an invitation arrived for Hans Luther to attend the first mass his son would perform, Hans declared, "Martin shall have no cause to be ashamed of his father!" With a company of twenty horsemen, Hans Luther came riding in, wearing his finest clothes, and made a large donation to the monastery.[12]

Martin Luther presided over the mass skillfully, with the greatest attention to every detail and without any apparent nervousness until he came to the words of consecration. Luther wholeheartedly believed that with those words the bread and wine were changed into the actual body and blood of Christ. Luther later remarked:

> *At these words I was utterly stupefied and terror-stricken. I thought to myself, "With what tongue shall I address such Majesty, seeing that all men ought to tremble in the presence of even an earthly prince? Who am I, that I should lift up mine eyes or raise my hands to the divine Majesty? The angels surround him. At his nod the earth trembles. And shall I, a miserable little pygmy, say, 'I want this, I ask for that'? For I am dust and ashes and full of sin and I am speaking to the living, eternal, and the true God."*[13]

Luther trembled greatly at these thoughts. For Martin Luther, this feeling of terror before God during the consecration had as profound an effect upon his soul as his earlier crisis of nearly being hit by lightning.

After his first mass, there was a feast. Martin Luther, still full of great concern for his soul, asked Hans, "Dear Father, why were you so contrary to my becoming a monk? And perhaps you are not satisfied even now. The life is so quiet and godly."

This was too much for old Hans, who had been doing his best to put aside his disappointment. He flared up before the monks and the guests, exclaiming, "You learned scholar, have you never read in the Bible that you should honor your father and mother? And here you have left me and your dear mother to look after ourselves in our old age!"

"But Father," Martin Luther replied, "I could do you more good by prayers than if I had stayed in the world." Then he related how he believed that God had called him to be a monk through his close brush with the lightning bolt.

"God grant," said Hans, "it was not an apparition of the Devil!"[14]

In 1510, Martin Luther and one other monk from Erfurt were chosen to transport letters to and from Rome. After a months-long journey by foot, Martin Luther finally stepped over the crest of the last hill leading to the Eternal City. At the first sight of Rome, Luther fell to his knees and cried out, "Hail, holy Rome!"

Luther spent a month in Rome. He fulfilled business for his monastery and he participated in the regular devotions of the Augustinian cloister where he was lodged. But he also spent as much time as possible visiting the holy relics.

The holy relics were the tombs of especially religious people, their bodily remains (John the Baptist's skull, for example), or other artifacts that people thought had religious significance (such as pieces of wood reportedly from the cross of Christ).

Luther had been taught that saying a prayer before these relics would reduce the time in purgatory for a deceased relative. (According to Roman Catholic teaching, "purgatory" is the place where the souls of Christians go to have their sins burned away before they can enter Heaven.) While Luther was in Rome, earning so much time off from purgatory for praying before the relics, he regretted that his parents were not yet dead and in purgatory so that he could lessen the years of suffering they might experience. (People thought that praying before the relics in Rome could only lessen the time in purgatory for those who were already dead.) Since his parents were still living, Luther dedicated his pilgrimage to his deceased grandparents.[15]

Luther was distressed at the general immorality he saw in Rome, and he was especially troubled by the lack of spirituality in the clergy (those who worked for the church). These church leaders rushed the people through their prayers in front of the relics so that they could move as many people through as possible. In this way, they received a greater amount of donations.

Luther experienced an intense crisis of faith upon ascending the *scala sancta*: the "sacred stairs." (People thought that long ago St. Helena, the mother of Emperor Constantine, had moved these stairs from Pilate's palace in Jerusalem to Rome.) Martin Luther ascended these stairs upon his knees, in the traditional manner. He repeated a prayer on each stair and kissed each one in the hope of delivering the souls of his grandparents from purgatory. Yet when he reached the top, Luther's mind was filled with doubt. He rose, looked back down at the crowds of kneeling, earnest pilgrims, and said aloud to himself, "Who knows whether it is so?"[16]

**Focus Verse**: But to him who does not work, but who believes in the one who justifies the impious, his faith is credited as righteousness (Romans 4:5).

## Questions for Reflection and Discussion

1. Why did Martin Luther's activities as a monk fail to give him peace?

2. How would you describe the Roman Catholic doctrine of purgatory?

3. What do you think Martin Luther meant when he asked himself, "Who knows whether it is so?" at the top of the *scala sancta*?

Martin Luther as a Monk

# Chapter 3

## Professorship in Wittenberg and Evangelical Experience

Martin Luther first taught at the University of Wittenberg during the winter semester of 1508-9. Johann von Staupitz, Luther's mentor, urged him to take this teaching position.[17] In the spring of 1511, upon returning from Rome, Luther was called by the Elector of Saxony—Frederick the Wise—to a permanent teaching position at the University of Wittenberg.[18] At first Luther taught Philosophy, then he transferred to teaching Theology. In time, Luther began to lecture through various books of the Bible. While he was getting ready for these lectures on Scripture, Luther finally came to a breakthrough in his understanding of justification.

The exact time of Martin Luther's spiritual rebirth (John 3:3,7) is a matter of some scholarly debate. What is certain is that Luther experienced a heart change as he was studying the book of Romans.[19] Luther later described his Reformation breakthrough as follows:

> *I greatly longed to understand Paul's Epistle to the Romans and nothing stood in the way but that one expression, "the justice of God."*

*because I took it to mean that justice by which God is just and deals justly in punishing the unjust. My situation was that, although an impeccable monk, I stood before God as a sinner troubled in conscience, and I had no confidence that my merit would assuage him. Therefore I did not love a just and angry God, but rather hated and murmured against him. Yet I clung to the dear Paul and had a great yearning to know what he meant.*

*Night and day I pondered until I saw the connection between the justice of God and the statement that "the just shall live by faith." Then I grasped that the justice of God is that righteousness by which through grace and sheer mercy God justifies us through faith. Thereupon I felt myself to be reborn and to have gone through open doors into paradise. The whole of Scripture took on a new meaning, and whereas before the "justice of God" had filled me with hate, now it became to me inexpressibly sweet in greater love. This passage of Paul became to me a gate to heaven...*

*Now this alone is the right Christian way, that I turn away from my sin and want nothing more to do with it, and turn alone to Christ's righteousness, so that I know for certain his goodness, merit, innocence, and holiness are mine, as surely as I know that this body is mine. In his name I live, die, and pass away, for he died for us and was resurrected for us. I am not good and just, but Christ is... he will embrace us if only we trust in him. [Luther's Works 34:336-338.]*[20]

For years, Martin Luther had been greatly worried over the question of whether he would be accepted or condemned before God on the Day of Judgment. He had tried to find peace through becoming a monk; he had tried to ease his mind about the peace of his family through praying before the relics in Rome. Through wrestling with the text of Romans 1:17, Luther finally came to find peace before God.[21] Though some of Luther's beliefs would certainly change over the years, the foundations for his core beliefs concerning the good news of Jesus Christ were evident from the moment of his conversion. *Scripture alone*– and not the teachings of the pope or councils, nor the rules of his monastic order– had brought him peace before God. While his own good works and spiritual devotions as a monk had only brought him to a state in which his conscience was more and more upset by his sins, Luther found salvation by *grace alone* through *faith alone* in *Christ alone*, on the basis of Jesus' righteousness on his behalf.

**Focus Verse**: For in [the gospel] the righteousness of God is revealed from faith unto faith, just as it has been written, "The just man by faith will live" (Romans 1:17).

## Questions for Reflection and Discussion

1. What was Martin Luther doing when he "felt [him]self to be reborn"?

2. According to Martin Luther, what does "the justice of God" mean in Romans 1? (Explain this in your own words.)

3. *Why* had Martin Luther's own good works and spiritual devotions only made him feel more guilty, rather than giving him peace?

Martin Luther Studying Scripture

# Chapter 4

## Background to the 95 Theses

It is likely that very few people would know the name "Martin Luther" today if Luther had not begun teaching against indulgences. Martin Luther became internationally famous due to the debate that was started when he argued against indulgences. Therefore, in order to understand the ministry of Martin Luther, it is extremely important to understand indulgences along with the Roman Catholic teachings connected to the sale of them and Luther's protest against those sales.

According to the *Catholic Encyclopedia*, "An indulgence is a remission of the temporal punishment due to sin, the guilt of which has been forgiven."[22] People believed that by earning or buying an indulgence from the Roman Catholic Church—or by having someone else earn or buy it on their behalf— they could be declared "not guilty" for some or all of their sins (depending on what type of indulgence was earned or bought). This was seen as a way to lessen the time spent in purgatory. In 1323 Pope Clement VI had issued official teaching concerning the "treasury of merits." The idea of indulgences was based on this teaching. Clement VI taught that Christ's life and the lives of saints provided an "overflow of merits." ("Merit" meaning "a reward for a good work.") These merits by the saints that go beyond their own needs are known as *supererogation.*

The *New Schaff-Herzog Encyclopedia* says concerning "Supererogation:"

> The sum total of the merits of Christ was greater than was required for the salvation of man, and that the saints also had done more and suffered more than was absolutely required to insure their own salvation, that these superabundant merits were placed in the "spiritual treasury" of the Church, at the disposal of its visible head [that is, the pope]; that as the Church is one, in this world and the next, they may be applied to such of its members as are still lacking in the required amount of works necessary to satisfy the divine demands.[23]

One way to access the "treasury of merits," according to the Catholic Church of Luther's day, was through indulgences granted in connection with gazing upon the relics of the saints. Frederick the Wise, who ruled the section of Germany in which Luther lived, and who founded the University of Wittenberg where Luther taught, had gathered a huge collection of relics. This collection was opened to the public on All Saints' Day.[24] By seeing Frederick's relics (after paying a fee), people thought they could reduce their time in purgatory by thousands of years.

Another way to access the "treasury of merits" was through other indulgences, which were issued in order to help people meet the "requirements of satisfaction" (works that showed repentance). These indulgences were supposed to free Christians from the guilt of daily sins as well as time in purgatory when normal means could not be used. Roland Bainton notes:

> At first indulgences were conferred on those who sacrificed or risked their lives in fighting against the infidel [that is, the Muslim people], and then were extended to those who, unable to go to the Holy Land [as Crusaders], made contributions to the enterprise. The device proved so lucrative [that is, the selling of indulgences made so much money] that it was speedily extended to cover the construction of churches, monasteries, and hospitals.[25]

While Luther was a professor in Wittenberg, Pope Leo X gave authority for a special indulgence in order to fund another bishopric for Albert of Mainz.

According to church rules at the time, a person could only become bishop over one area (the area over which a person is bishop is known as a "bishopric"). Somehow Albert of Mainz had gotten around the rules and had obtained two bishoprics already (thus receiving double the offering money from the churches under his "care"). When he asked Leo X for a third bishopric, Leo X granted his request, provided that Albert pay him a large fee. In order to secure this fee, Albert had to borrow money from Jakob Fugger, who was one of the wealthiest individuals of all time. So that he could repay Jakob Fugger, Albert asked Leo X to authorize a special indulgence that could be sold in his bishoprics. The money from sales of this special indulgence would be divided in two. Part of the money would go to Albert, so that he could repay Jakob Fugger; the other part of the money would go to Pope Leo X, so that he could fund renovations to St. Peter's Basilica in Rome. The special indulgence was said to offer four benefits for Christians who purchased it:

☐ The plenary remission of sins (that is, the punishment for all the purchaser's sins would be turned back; this was usually taken to mean that anyone who bought this indulgence for his or her own sake would not have to spend time in purgatory);

☐  A confessional letter allowing the penitent to choose his confessor (that is, if a person did not want to confess sins to his or her own priest, buying this indulgence would allow for the purchaser to choose another priest);

☐  A share for one and one's family in all alms, fasts, prayers, and pilgrimages of every sort (that is, part of the merit earned by others performing spiritual deeds would be placed on the heavenly account of those who bought this indulgence);

☐  The total remission of all sins for souls in purgatory (that is, if a person bought this indulgence on behalf of a deceased Christian, that Christian was thought to be immediately released from purgatory into Heaven).[26]

Johan Tetzel, a priest of the Dominican order, was the most infamous indulgence salesman. Indulgence preachers would often set up a replica of the papal seal [the symbol of the pope] to indicate that they were under the pope's authority. Tetzel would set up this seal in the town square wherever he went and cry out to the people gathered there. In order to get people to purchase indulgences, he would use unscrupulous tactics. One such tactic involved calling to mind the deceased family members of his hearers. He would claim that the deceased family members were writhing in agony in the fires of purgatory while the living family members held the money that could set them free. The following are quotes from Tetzel:

> *Listen to the voices of your dear dead relatives and friends, beseeching you and saying, 'Pity us, pity us. We are in dire torment from which you can redeem us for a pittance.' Do you not wish to? Open your ears. Hear the father saying to his son, the mother to her daughter, 'We bore you, nourished you, brought you up, left you our fortunes, and you are so cruel and hard that now you are not willing for so little to set us free. Will you let us lie here in flames? Will you delay our promised glory?*[27]

> *Remember that you are able to release them, for as soon as the coin in the coffer rings, the soul from purgatory springs. Will you not then for a quarter of a florin receive these letters of indulgence through which you are able to lead a divine and immortal soul into the fatherland of paradise?*[28]

> *You priest, you nobleman, you merchant, you woman, you virgin, you married woman, you youth, you old man, go into*

*your church, which, as I have said, is St. Peter's, and visit the hallowed cross that has been put up for you, that incessantly calls you... You should know: whoever has confessed and is contrite and puts alms into the box, as his confessor counsels him, will have all of his sins forgiven, and even after confession and after the jubilee year will acquire an indulgence on every day that he visits the cross and the altars, as if he were visiting the seven altars in the Church of St. Peter, where the perfect indulgence is granted.*[29]

Reports of Tetzel's extravagant statements prompted Luther to begin arguing against the way that indulgences were being sold.

**Focus Verse**: "So you also, when you have done all you were commanded, say, 'We are undeserving slaves; we have only done what we were supposed to do'" (Luke 17:10).

## Questions for Reflection and Discussion

1. According to the Roman Catholic Church, what is an "indulgence"?

2. According to the Roman Catholic Church, what is "supererogation"?

3. What four benefits were promised to those who bought the special indulgence sold in the bishoprics of Albert of Mainz?

Martin Luther Posting the 95 Theses

# Chapter 5

## Posting the 95 Theses

On October 31, 1517, Martin Luther posted the 95 Theses against indulgences on the door of Castle Church in Wittenberg. (In Luther's time, people used the door of the church building as a kind of bulletin board.) The Theses were written assertions that were meant to form the basis of debates for teachers in the university and in the church. The 95 Theses were originally written in Latin, and Luther seemed to think that only a few theologians would debate them. Two weeks after the 95 Theses were posted, however, they were translated into German and given to a printer. Soon, nearly everyone in Germany was discussing and debating the Theses.

The 95 Theses may be understood according to three main points:

1. "An objection to the avowed object of the expenditure" [that is, Luther objected to the idea that the pope can forgive sins];"
2. "A denial of the powers of the pope over purgatory;"
3. "A consideration of the welfare of the sinner."[30]

When Luther wrote the 95 Theses, he seems to have held the view that forgiveness of sins came through the ministry of priests who derived their authority from Rome. Luther later held opposing views against the pope and Roman Catholic teaching.[31] At this time, however, Luther upheld Roman authority, as seen in Thesis 7: "God remits guilt to no one whom He does not, at the same time, humble in all things and bring into subjection to His vicar, the priest."

Overall, the Theses seem to indicate that, when they were written, Luther still held to beliefs in:

1. Purgatory;
2. Indulgences (in some sense);
3. The pope.

On the other hand, Luther did interpret penance biblically rather than sacramentally, as seen in Thesis 4: "The penalty [of sin], therefore, continues so long as hatred of self continues; for this is the true inward repentance, and continues until our entrance into the kingdom of heaven." When he wrote the 95 Theses, Luther believed that penance involved a heart condition, rather than a ritual performed with a priest.

The 95 Theses denied three main points of Roman doctrine:

1. "There is no such thing as supererogation;"
2. "The pope has no jurisdiction over purgatory;"
3. "Peace comes in the word of Christ through faith. He who does not have this is lost even though he is absolved a million times by the pope..."[32]

At the time when he wrote the 95 Theses, Luther taught that repentance and faith are synonymous. It is interesting that indulgences were rarely mentioned in the Theses, but when he did mention them, Luther clearly stated that good works are better than indulgences (Theses 43 and 45). Concerning indulgences, Luther argued that papal authority is not to the extent that the pope may dispense or withhold grace. Luther's teaching of the superiority of repentance over indulgences was considered revolutionary, but this teaching was actually preceded by the writings of another Augustinian monk, Gottschalk Hollen, who declared in c.1452, "Repentance is better than indulgences."[33] In the background of the Theses, then, was the change in Luther's theology gained from his study of Pauline and Augustinian theology. He undertook these studies first as a monk, then as a university professor in Wittenberg.

When Luther began teaching against indulgences, many people who considered themselves faithful Catholics began listening to him. In Luther's day, the *doctrine* taught by the Catholic Church concerning indulgences was extremely vague. Uncertainty over the doctrine of indulgences led many Catholics to believe that they might agree with Luther's teaching against *practices* associated with the sale of indulgences.

When he posted the 95 Theses, Luther was not meaning to attack papal authority in general, but the *abuse* of the doctrine of indulgences. But many interpreted Luther's intention to discuss and debate as an attack on the power of the papacy. The Theses struck a blow at the misuse of indulgences and thereby simultaneously called into question a central position of Catholic piety: the authority of the pope. Questioning the indulgences instituted by the pope led others (and eventually Luther himself) to question the pope's authority in general.

**Focus Verse**: From then on, Jesus began to preach, saying, "Repent, for the kingdom of Heaven has come near!" (Matthew 4:17)

## Questions for Reflection and Discussion

1. What three main points was Martin Luther seeking to explore in the 95 Theses? (Explain these in your own words.)

2. What does it mean to interpret the word "penance" biblically rather than sacramentally?

3. Why did Martin Luther's teachings against indulgences lead others to question the authority of the pope?

Martin Luther's Interview with Cardinal Cajetan

# Chapter 6

# Interview With Cardinal Cajetan

As Luther's 95 Theses gained increasing popularity, the pope felt he must respond. His first response was to instruct the Augustinian order to deal with the matter, for Luther was one of its members. Justo Gonzales recounts:

> The Reformer was called to the next chapter meeting of the order, in Heidelberg. He went in fear for his life, for he expected to be condemned and burned as a heretic. But he was surprised to find that many of his fellow friars favored his teaching, and that some of the younger ones were even enthusiastic about it. Others saw the dispute between Luther and Tetzel as one more instance of the ancient rivalry between the Dominicans and Augustinians, and therefore refused to abandon their champion. Eventually, Luther was able to return to Wittenberg, strengthened by the support of his order, and encouraged by those whom he had won for his cause.[34]

The pope then attempted to summon Luther to Rome, but Frederick the Wise "wrote a calming letter to the pope, pointing out that it was right for German citizens to be tried in their own country."[35]

Gonzales continues:

> The pope then took a different route. The Diet of the Empire—the assembly of princes and nobles—was scheduled to meet in Augsburg, under the presidence of Emperor Maximilian. As his legate to that gathering, Leo [X] sent Cardinal Cajetan, a man of vast erudition...[36]

The pope then sent a letter of safe passage for Luther, summoning him to appear before Cardinal Cajetan at the Diet of Augsburg. Cardinal Cajetan was tasked with getting Luther to recant. If Luther would not recant, Cajetan was to have him bound and sent to Rome. (Since the days of Jan Hus—who was burned at the stake for setting the authority of Scripture above the authority of the pope—church leaders understood that letters of safe passage were not valid in the case of notorious heretics. Notorious heretics were defined as those who were well-known for going against the teachings of the Catholic Church).

When Luther came before Cardinal Cajetan, he followed the protocol of prostrating himself before the Cardinal. Cajetan then warmly bade Luther to rise. It seems that the Cardinal fully expected to hear Luther utter a single word, *"Recanto,"* meaning, "I recant," after which Cajetan could offer Luther forgiveness. Instead, Luther asked to be instructed concerning his errors.

Bainton reports:

> The cardinal replied that the chief [error] was the denial of the Church's treasury of merit clearly enunciated [by] Pope Clement VI in the year 1343, "Here," said Cajetan, "you have a statement by the pope that the merits of Christ are a treasure of indulgences." Luther, who knew the text well, answered that he would recant if it said so. Cajetan chuckled, leafed through the page to the spot where it said Christ by his sacrifice acquired a treasure. "Oh, yes," said Luther, "but you said that the merits of Christ *are* a treasure. This says he *acquired* a treasure. To *be* and to *acquire* do not mean the same thing. You need not think we Germans are ignorant of grammar."[37]

Exact language is important, especially to theologians and Bible teachers, and Luther had a point in distinguishing between the words "are" and "acquire." The Roman Catholic view concerning the merits of Christ pictured them as a kind of treasure chest from which pardon for sins could be distributed by the pope and his appointed officers. Luther would argue that the merits of Christ "acquired a treasure." He maintained that the perfect life, substitutionary death, and glorious resurrection of Jesus provided everything sinners needed for salvation and godliness, without any regard to the actions of the pope.

Cajetan failed to appreciate this distinction:

> ..."My son," [Cajetan] snapped, "I did not come to wrangle with you. I am ready to reconcile you with the Roman Church." But since reconciliation was possible only through recantation, Luther protested that he ought not be condemned unheard and unrefuted. "I am not conscious," said he, "of going against Scripture, the fathers, the decretals, or right reason."[38]

Luther asked for a council to be convened in order to determine whether his teaching was in line with Scripture, but Cardinal Cajetan replied, "The pope is above a council, above everything in the Church."[39]

"His Holiness abuses Scripture," retorted Luther, "I deny that he is above Scripture."[40] Cajetan then angrily had Luther thrown out of his meeting-place, warning Luther not to come back until he was ready to recant.

That night Staupitz released Luther from his Augustinian vows. Staupitz apparently took this action both to protect the Augustinians from any reprisals by Rome and to guard Luther's conscience from the guilt of vow-breaking. Fearing that he would be bound and sent to Rome in order to be burned as a heretic (as he certainly would have been), Luther escaped from Augsburg in the middle of the night.

**Focus Verse**: He who did not spare even his own Son, but gave him up for the sake of us all, how will he not also with him grant us all things? (Romans 8:32)

## Questions for Reflection and Discussion

1. Why did the pope (and his followers) feel justified in their apparent plans to burn Martin Luther as a heretic?

2. Why did Martin Luther refuse to say *recanto*– "I recant"– when saying that one word would have gotten him out of trouble?

3. What authority is above the pope, according to Martin Luther?

John Eck

# Chapter 7

# The Leipzig Disputation and the Papal Bull

For various political reasons, after Martin Luther's interview with Cardinal Cajetan, Pope Leo X sought a more conciliatory relationship with Luther. Leo X sent an emissary, Carl von Miltitz, to Frederick the Wise. Von Miltitz was a cousin of Frederick. Miltitz spoke with Luther, and secured Luther's promise that he would no longer engage in debate and publication regarding indulgences, if those within the Catholic Church who had been opposing Luther would likewise refrain from attacking his position.

This truce was short-lived, however, due to the actions of John Eck. Eck, a professor at the University of Ingolstadt, had already engaged in public debate with Luther through a publication titled *Obelisks*, which was intended to refute the 95 Theses. Eck had persuaded Duke George the Bearded of Saxony to sponsor a debate between himself and Andreas Carlstadt–a Wittenberg professor who had become convinced of Luther's teachings–at the University of Leipzig. Luther desired to defend his own teachings, and so he arranged to debate Eck at Leipzig as well.

In July 1519, after Eck and Carlstadt debated for a week concerning the radical sinfulness of humanity.[41] After that debate Luther debated Eck on the question of whether the papacy was of divine or human institution. According to the terms of the debate, neither Luther nor Eck could bring books to the table, but they were dependent upon what they had memorized. The proof quoted by Eck consisted of canon law and selections from church history. Though Luther had studied vigorously for the debate, he was no match for Eck in regards to these types of documents. Luther instinctively turned to the writings that he had memorized for years as a monk and as a professor of theology. In response to Eck, Luther quoted the Bible.

Luther's quoting the Bible to refute canon law brought the charge from Eck that Luther was a Hussite (a follower of the teachings of Jan Hus), since Jan Hus had similarly argued against the papacy on the basis of Scripture. Luther objected to the charge, saying that Hus should have kept to the unity of the Church, but as the debate went on it became apparent that Luther had only a vague knowledge concerning what Hus had actually taught. At the lunch break, Luther retreated to the library to study documents from the Council of Constance: the assembly at which Hus had been condemned. As Luther studied Hus's words from the Council of Constance, he was surprised at what he found. Luther was especially surprised to find that Hus, even in taking actions that further fragmented the institutional Catholic Church, actually quoted Augustine in affirming that there is only one Church, spiritually speaking. This one Church was made of all those whom God had chosen for salvation. When the debate continued, Luther affirmed, "Among the articles of John Hus, I find many which are plainly Christian and evangelical, which the universal Church cannot condemn."[42] This statement greatly troubled Duke George, who viewed the Hussites as political enemies of the Saxons.

Luther used the Leipzig Disputation to refine his doctrine of *sola Scriptura. Sola Scriptura* is the understanding of Scripture alone as the final and sufficient authority concerning matters of life and godliness for the individual believer and the Church as a whole. During the debate, Luther asserted:

> *[A] council has sometimes erred and may sometimes err. Nor has a council authority to establish new articles of faith. A council cannot make divine right out of that which by nature is not divine right. Councils have contradicted each other, for the recent Lateran Council has reversed the claim of the councils of Constance and Basel that a council is above a pope. A simple layman*

*armed with Scripture is to be believed above a pope or a council without it. As for the pope's decretal on indulgences, I say that neither the Church nor the pope can establish articles of faith. These must come from Scripture. For the sake of Scripture we should reject pope and councils.*[43]

In 1520, Martin Luther published five of his primary works: *The Sermon on Good Works* in May, *The Papacy at Rome* in June, *The Address to the German Nobility* in August, *The Babylonian Captivity* in September, and *The Freedom of the Christian Man* in November.[44] Luther's teachings in these works were directly informed by the insight he gained concerning *sola Scriptura* during the Leipzig Disputation.

Pope Leo X, meanwhile, despaired of conciliation with Luther based on the reports he heard from the Leipzig Disputation. He was further troubled by Luther's affirmation of Hus (whom the pope considered a heretic), so he issued a papal bull titled *Exsurge Domine*. In this document, the pope proclaimed that if Luther did not recant, he would be excommunicated.[45] Whenever a copy of the papal bull reached a new town, those in the town who were faithful to the pope would hurl all of the publications by Luther that they could find into a bonfire. Receiving reports concerning the contents of the bull, Luther eventually published two tracts in response: *Against the Execrable Bull of the Antichrist* and *Assertion of all the Articles Wrongly Condemned in the Roman Bull.*

At 10 A.M. on December 10, 1520, the faculty and students of the University of Wittenberg joined by many citizens from the town who agreed with Luther met at a large bonfire. Here they tossed volumes of papal constitutions, canon law, and works of scholastic theology into the fire. Luther himself flung a copy of the papal bull on the flames.

**Focus Verse:** Every Scripture is God-breathed and is profitable for teaching, for rebuking, for correcting, and for training in righteousness, so that the man of God may be complete, equipped for every good work. (2 Timothy 3:16-17)

## Questions for Reflection and Discussion

1. According to John Hus and Martin Luther, what is the Church?

2. What authority is above a council, according to Martin Luther?

3. What proof does Martin Luther give for his assertion that a church council cannot be considered as the highest authority for a Christian?

Martin Luther at the Diet of Worms

# Chapter 8

## The Diet of Worms

In 1521, Martin Luther faced the trial that became known as the most significant public test of his faith. Luther was summoned to appear before the Diet of Worms over which Charles V–Emperor of the Holy Roman Empire–presided. Charles V convened the Diet of Worms for the purpose of consolidating his power against his enemies: the governments of France and the Ottoman Empire. Charles V viewed the controversy over Luther's teachings as a threat to the unity of the Holy Roman Empire. He wished to determine whether any agreement could be found between the Lutherans and the Romanists. No agreement would be reached at the Diet, however, because from the Roman point of view Luther needed to recant his teachings. Luther's point of view, on the other hand, was that the pope and his followers needed to repent of their teachings. For Charles V, the Diet of Worms was a move in a political game. For Luther and his opponents, the Diet of Worms was a battlefield for spiritual warfare.

Luther was scheduled to appear at 4PM on April 17, 1521 before a committee of the Diet. The streets of Worms were choked with crowds of both

Luther's supporters and his opponents, and so the soldiers escorting Luther had to bring him to the Diet through a rear entrance. Luther then had to wait in a vestibule for about two hours as the committee considered other business. Finally appearing before the committee, Luther was confronted by a table on which his books were piled. Johan Eck, an official representing the Archbishop of Trier (no relation to the Eck of the Leipzig Disputation), addressed Luther as follows:

> *Dr. Martin Luther, you have been called before His Imperial Majesty in regard to certain doctrines that you have seen fit to propound and scatter; doctrines that have been judged to be heresy by His Holiness, the pope, the Most Blessed Father, Leo the Tenth. You have been called here to state whether these books arranged on this table were written by you, and whether you are prepared to recant the heresy they contain.*[46]

Luther was about to answer when his counsel spoke:

> *Would it please you to have the titles of the books read in order that Dr. Luther might*

*know whether or not he is the author of each?*[47]

Eck agreed. As he picked up each book and read its title, Luther acknowledged by a nod of his head that he was the author. When all were read, Eck turned again and addressed Luther:

*Having acknowledged that you are the author of all these books, you are now asked to declare whether you are ready to recant the heretical doctrines that they contain. What do you say?*[48]

Luther reflected aloud:

*This touches God and his Word. This affects the salvation of souls. Of this Christ said, "he who denies me before men, him I will deny before my father." To say too little or too much would be dangerous. I beg you, give me time to think it over.*[49]

Bainton notes:

The emperor and the diet deliberated. Eck brought the answer. He expressed amazement that a theological professor should not be ready at once to defend his position, particularly since he had come for that very purpose. He deserved no consideration. Nevertheless, the emperor in his clemency would grant him until the morrow.[50]

Luther's delay in answering whether he would recant had the effect of allowing him to appear before a plenary session of the Diet rather than before a committee.[51]

On April 18 Luther was once again scheduled to appear before the Diet at 4PM, and once again business of the Diet delayed his appearance for about two hours.

Eck asked Luther if he was ready to recant, to which Luther responded:

*Most serene emperor, most illustrious princes, most clement lords, if I have not given some of you your proper titles I beg you to forgive me. I am not a courtier, but a monk. You asked me yesterday whether [these books were all mine and whether] I would repudiate them. They are all mine, but as for the second question, they are not all of one sort... Some deal with faith and life so simply and evangelically that my very enemies are compelled to regard them as worthy of Christian reading. Even the bull itself does not treat all my books as of one kind. If I should renounce these, I would be the only man on earth to damn the truth confessed alike by my friends and foes. A second class of my works inveighs against the desolation of the Christian world by the evil lives and teachings of the papists. Who can deny this when the universal complaints testify that by the laws of the popes the consciences of men are racked?*[52]

"No!" broke in the emperor.

But Luther continued:

*Should I recant at this point, I would open the door to more tyranny and impiety, and it will be all the worse should it appear that I had done so at the instance of the Holy Roman Empire...*

*A third class contains attacks on private individuals. I confess that I have been more caustic than comports with my profession, but I am being judged, not on my life, but for the teaching of Christ, and I cannot renounce these works either, without increasing tyranny and impiety. When Christ stood before Ananias, he said, 'Produce witnesses.' If our Lord, who could not err, made this demand, why may not a worm like me ask to be convicted of error from the prophets and the Gospels? If I am shown my error, I will be first to throw my books into the fire. I have been reminded of the dissensions which my teaching engenders. I can answer only in the words of the Lord, 'I came not to bring peace but a sword.' If our God is so severe, let us beware lest we release a deluge of wars, lest the reign of this noble youth, Charles, be inauspicious. Take warning from the examples of Pharaoh, the king of Babylon, and the kings of Israel. God it is who confounds the wise. I must walk in the fear of the Lord. I say this not to chide but because I cannot escape my duty to my Germans. I commend myself to Your Majesty. May you not suffer my adversaries to make you ill-disposed to me without cause. I have spoken.*[53]

Eck replied:

*Martin, you have not sufficiently distinguished your works. The earlier were bad and the latter worse. Your plea to be heard from Scripture is the one always made by heretics. You do nothing but renew the errors of Wyclif and Hus. How will the Jews, how will the Turks, exult to hear Christians discussing whether they have been wrong all these years! Martin, how can you assume that you are the only one to understand the sense of Scripture? Would you put your judgment above that of so many famous men and claim that you know more than they all? You have no right to call into question the most holy and orthodox faith, instituted by Christ the perfect lawgiver, proclaimed through the world by the apostles, sealed by the red blood of the martyrs, confirmed by the sacred councils, defined by the Church in which all our fathers believed until death and gave to us as an inheritance, and which now we are forbidden by the pope and the emperor to discuss lest there be no end of debate. I ask you, Martin—answer candidly and without horns—do you or do you not repudiate your books and the errors which they contain?*[54]

Luther replied:

*Since then Your Majesty and your lordships
desire a simple reply, I will answer without
horns and without teeth. Unless I am convicted
by Scripture and by plain reason—I do not
accept the authority of popes and councils,
for they have contradicted each other; my
conscience is captive to the Word of God—I
cannot and will not recant anything, for to
go against conscience is neither right nor
safe... Here I stand, I cannot do otherwise...
God help me, Amen.*[55]

Luther, who had been speaking in German, was
asked to repeat what he had said in Latin, which he
did. Then Luther raised his arms victoriously and
departed for his hotel.

Charles V was eager to be known as a just ruler,
and so he honored his promise of Luther's safe
passage and allowed him to depart for Wittenberg.
But Charles V was also eager to be known as a
faithful Roman Catholic. He was greatly concerned
that Luther's challenge of religious authority would
result in a challenge to political authority as well,
thus undermining his own rule. Therefore, Emperor
Charles V issued the Edict of Worms, declaring Luther
a "notorious heretic." The Edict of Worms called on

the citizens of the Holy Roman Empire to both destroy all of Luther's works and to capture Luther himself so that he may be punished as a heretic (i.e., he was to be burned at the stake).

Now Luther had been declared a heretic by both the Pope of the Roman Catholic Church and the Emperor of the Holy Roman Empire.

**Focus Verse**: "But whoever denies me before men, I will also deny him before my Father who is in Heaven" (Matthew 10:33).

## Questions for Reflection and Discussion

1. Why did Martin Luther ask for time to think over whether he would recant?

2. Has your faith ever been tested? How?

3. What did Martin Luther mean by his statement, "Here I stand, I cannot do otherwise"?

Martin Luther as "Sir George"

# Chapter 9

## "Sir George"

On the way back to Wittenberg from the Diet of Worms, the wagon bearing Luther, his friend Amsdorf, and several other companions was attacked by a band of ferocious men. Luther was dragged to the ground and was placed on horseback, then surrounded by the ruffians, who hurried him off into the woods. The other men who had been traveling with Luther quickly spread the word of his abduction. For a time, virtually no-one knew whether Luther was alive or dead.

But Frederick the Wise was confident that Luther was safe. Justifiably concerned for Luther's well-being following the Diet, Frederick had instructed certain of his court officials to hide Luther away. Frederick had remained intentionally ignorant of the location to which Luther would be taken. If anyone asked him, he could honestly say that he had no idea where Luther was.

In the middle of the night, Luther was brought by a circuitous route to Wartburg Castle outside of Eisenach. Luther was confined to the Castle (and its immediate grounds) for a period of months, with only a warden and two serving boys for company. At the castle, Luther suffered physically from insomnia and severe constipation. He also suffered spiritually from doubts and fears. These fears were intensified as he received news from Wittenberg concerning certain developments in the church reforms there.

Philip Melanchthon, Luther's closest friend, had continued Luther's efforts in religious reform at Wittenberg. Melanchthon was assisted by Gabriel Zwilling (a monk from Luther's Augustinian order) and by Andreas Carlstadt (a fellow professor at the University of Wittenberg, who had been Luther's debate partner against John Eck at the Leipzig Disputation). Zwilling and Carlstadt were more radical than Melanchthon Through their influence priests, monks, and nuns abandoned their vows of celibacy in favor of marriage, common people took up the elements of communion with their own hands (rather than having the priests place the communion wafer on their tongue), and statues of saints were destroyed. Luther approved of many of these changes, but the spirit with which they were being executed troubled him. Townspeople harassed pilgrims who were on their way to see the relics of the saints and threw stones at those who were saying private devotions in church to the Virgin Mary.

On December 4, 1521, Luther returned to Wittenberg in disguise.[56] Luther had grown out his beard, was dressed in knight's clothing, and introduced himself as Sir George. Luther was pleased with the advances made by Melanchthon, Zwilling, Carlstadt, and others, but he found the reports concerning violence to be confirmed as well (there was a riot in Wittenberg the day before Luther arrived). Upon returning to Wartburg Castle, Luther wrote letters warning his supporters that violence would not aid the spread of the gospel: that it would only aid the cause of the Reformation's enemies. A few months later, the Wittenberg City Council, feeling the need for Luther's leadership, sent a formal letter to Luther, requesting that he return from hiding. Luther accepted the request and sent notice to Frederick the Wise of his intention to return. Frederick urged Luther not to return, saying that he could not guarantee Luther's safety without risking all-out war with the Empire. Luther replied to Frederick that he was depending on God's protection alone. (Luther later sent a letter to the Imperial Diet of Nurnberg testifying that Frederick had nothing to do with his return to Wittenberg.)

On his return trip to Wittenberg, Luther stopped at the Black Bear Inn outside the city of Jena, still disguised as Sir George. As Luther sat studying at a table in the dining area, two men entered from out of the storm. Luther hospitably invited the men to share a drink with him. Learning that the men were travelers from Switzerland, he asked them what the

Swiss thought concerning Dr. Luther. Perceiving that the knight seemed favorably disposed toward Luther, the men confided that they were traveling to Wittenberg with hopes of studying under Luther. They asked the "knight" whether he knew if Luther was currently in Wittenberg. "I know quite positively that he is not," Luther replied, "but he will be shortly." After Luther left the room, the Swiss travelers pondered over the fact that the book Sir George had been studying appeared to be written in Hebrew. The innkeeper, having overheard their conversation, and realizing that they were supporters of Martin Luther, informed them that "Sir George" was actually Luther himself. The Swiss travelers could not believe their ears, and they imagined that the innkeeper had said "Hutten" (a well-known German knight at the time). They were quite surprised when they later met Luther in Wittenberg![57]

Upon returning to Wittenberg, Luther preached a series of sermons emphasizing the fruit of the Spirit and warning against violence.

During his time at Wartburg Castle, Luther had written almost a dozen books, numerous tracts, and (most significantly) he translated the New Testament into German.

**Focus Verse**: "Look, I'm sending you as sheep in the midst of wolves therefore be shrewd as snakes and innocent as doves" (Matthew 10:16).

## Questions for Reflection and Discussion

1. Why did Frederick's men pretend to kidnap Martin Luther?

2. Why did Martin Luther experience so much suffering while he was at Wartburg Castle?

3. What did Martin Luther accomplish while he was at Wartburg Castle? Do you think he could have accomplished these tasks if he had not been in hiding? (Why or why not?)

Martin Luther's Wife: Katharina von Bora

# Chapter 10

# Marriage and Family Life

While Luther was in hiding at Wartburg Castle, priests, monks, and nuns who were persuaded of evangelical teaching began abandoning their vows of celibacy in favor of marriage. Luther, in the main, came to approve of this move. Initially, however, Luther–who had been a monk for so long–could not imagine being married. He exclaimed, "Good heavens! They won't give me a wife."[58]

Resistance to taking a wife for himself, however, did not exempt Luther from becoming entangled in the marriage plans of others. Priests, monks, and nuns who left their vows generally had no other source of income and no social standing. Those who had been persuaded to leave their vows through reading Luther's books and tracts now came to look to Luther for help in beginning their new lives by helping them find spouses.

In 1521 Martin Luther wrote a book titled *The Judgment of Martin Luther on Monastic Vows* in which he argued, "Nowhere does the Bible teach that men and women should withdraw from the world to lonely monasteries and convents."[59]Two years later, a small group of nuns from the Nimbschen

Convent sent Luther a letter asking for his help so that they might escape their captivity and follow their consciences concerning God's Word. Sneaking nuns out of their convent was no small matter, as such an action was considered a crime worthy of the death penalty. Luther, however, enlisted the aid of Leonard Kopp, a brave, elderly gentleman who occasionally delivered barrels of pickled herring to the convent. And so, on the night before Easter, 1523, twelve nuns left Nimbschen Convent in a covered wagon, secreted among the fish-barrels.

Three of the nuns were able to return to their families, and so nine young ladies eventually arrived in Wittenberg. Six of the former nuns were wed rather quickly. Then two more were wed. Luther had sought to match the last, Katharina von Bora, with Jerome Baumgartner, a former student at the University of Wittenberg. However, Baumgartner's family had objected to him marrying a former nun, and he ended up marrying a woman of considerable wealth. Next, Luther tried to match von Bora with Dr. Kaspar Glatz, whom she was unwilling to marry. Katharina confided to Luther's friend Amsdorf that she would be willing to marry either him or Dr. Luther. Neither Amsdorf nor Luther intended to marry, due (primarily) to their work with the Reformation. They believed that their work was all-consuming, which would prevent them from fulfilling their duties as husbands, and that they were likely to die as martyrs.

Luther changed his mind about marriage due to the influence of his parents, who desired for him to father their grandchildren. In defending his decision to ask Katharina von Bora to marry him, Luther said that he would marry in order "to please his father [who wanted him to help pass on the family name through fathering children], to spite the pope and the Devil [as the pope had forbidden priests, monks, and nuns, from leaving their vows to pursue marriage], and to seal his witness before martyrdom [his witness that he trusted in God to provide]."[60]

Martin Luther ultimately married Katharina von Bora out of concern for her, for his parents, and for his ministry. He did not marry based on romantic love, as he confessed, "I am not infatuated."[61] Martin and Katharina were married on the evening of June 13, 1525 at Luther's house, in the presence of a small group of friends. They had a larger wedding ceremony on June 27, 1525 at which Luther's parents and Leonard Kopp, among many others, were present.[62]

Despite Luther's initial lack of romantic feeling toward Katharina, his letters to his wife and other friends paint the picture of a tender, affectionate home-life. Martin referred to Katharina as "my dear Katie" and jokingly as "Lord Katie." Martin praised Katharina for her abilities to manage the

Luther household, which included her aunt, two of her nieces, many visitors, and eventually six children (though two of Luther's daughters, to the great grief of the family, died at quite a young age). By all accounts, the Luthers sought to live in accordance with what Martin had previously written in *The Estate of Marriage* (1521):

> Now observe that when that clever harlot, our natural reason (which the pagans followed in trying to be most clever), takes a look at married life, she turns up her nose and says, "Alas, must I rock the baby, wash its diapers, make its bed, smell its stench, stay up nights with it, take care of it when it cries, heal its rashes and sores, and on top of that care for my wife, provide for her, labour at my trade, take care of this and take care of that, do this and do that, endure this and endure that, and whatever else of bitterness and drudgery married life involves? What, should I make such a prisoner of myself? O you poor, wretched fellow, have you taken a wife? Fie, fie upon such wretchedness and bitterness! It is better to remain free and lead a peaceful, carefree life; I will become a priest or a nun and compel my children to do likewise." What then does Christian faith

say to this? It opens its eyes, looks upon all these insignificant, distasteful, and despised duties in the Spirit, and is aware that they are all adorned with divine approval as with the costliest gold and jewels. It says, "O God, because I am certain that thou hast created me as a man and hast from my body begotten this child, I also know for a certainty that it meets with thy perfect pleasure. I confess to thee that I am not worthy to rock the little babe or wash its diapers, or to be entrusted with the care of the child and its mother. How is it that I, without any merit, have come to this distinction of being certain that I am serving thy creature and thy most precious will? O how gladly will I do so, though the duties should be even more insignificant and despised. Neither frost nor heat, neither drudgery nor labour, will distress or dissuade me, for I am certain that it is thus pleasing in thy sight.

A wife too should regard her duties in the same light, as she suckles the child, rocks and bathes it, and cares for it in other ways; and as she busies herself with other duties and renders help and obedience to her husband. These are truly golden and noble works. . . .

Now you tell me, when a father goes ahead and washes diapers or performs some other mean task for his child, and someone ridicules him as an effeminate fool, though that father is acting in the spirit just described and in Christian faith, my dear fellow you tell me, which of the two is most keenly ridiculing the other? God, with all his angels and creatures, is smiling, not because that father is washing diapers, but because he is doing so in Christian faith. Those who sneer at him and see only the task but not the faith are ridiculing God with all his creatures, as the biggest fool on earth. Indeed, they are only ridiculing themselves; with all their cleverness they are nothing but devil's fools.[63]

**Focus Verse**: Husbands, love your wives, just as Christ loved the Church and gave himself up for her. (Ephesians 5:25)

## Questions for Reflection and Discussion

1. Why was Martin Luther, at first, against the idea of his getting married?

2. Why did Martin Luther eventually agree to marry Katharina von Bora?

3. Why did Martin Luther call caring for small children "truly golden and noble works"?

Martin Luther's Friend: Philip Melanchthon

# Chapter 11

# The Augsburg Confession

In 1526, Emperor Charles V called an imperial diet at Speyer for the purpose of trying to establish unity between the Roman Catholics and the Lutherans.[64] At this first Diet of Speyer, the German princes decided to suspend the Edict of Worms. They also "drew up a declaration stating that each was to live and rule his principality in such a way that he would not be afraid to answer to God for his actions."[65]

In 1529, a second Diet of Speyer took a different tack. At that point there was a renewed threat of imperial intervention within Germany, for the purpose of restoring order. Some German princes, who until then had been fairly moderate, joined the ranks of the staunch Catholics. They thought that if they reaffirmed their Roman Catholic faith the Emperor would not find grounds to lessen their authority. The result was that the Edict of Worms, which condemned Luther and his writings, was reaffirmed. This prompted the Lutheran princes to present a formal protest; these princes, and those who followed them in opposing the Roman Catholic Church for biblical reasons, were thereafter called "Protestants."[66]

In 1530 Emperor Charles V summoned an imperial diet to meet in Augsburg to restore religious unity to the empire.[67] At Worms, the emperor had refused to listen to Luther's arguments. But now, in view of the continued resistance of some German princes, and the emperor's urgent need to present a unified front against the Turkish Empire, he requested an orderly exposition of the points at issue.[68] The Protestants were asked for a summary statement of their position; Philip Melanchthon (1497-1560), Luther's friend and most prominent follower, drafted this summary of Protestant teaching.[69] This document that Melanchthon drafted is now known as the "Augsburg Confession." When first drawn, the Augsburg Confession was only intended to represent the teachings affirmed by the Protestants of Saxony. However, other princes and leaders also signed it, and so it became the instrument whereby most Protestants presented a united front before the emperor and the pope.[70]

Bainton notes:

> One might take the date June 25, 1530, the day when the Augsburg Confession was publicly read, as the death day of the Holy Roman Empire. From this day forward the two confessions [that of the Protestants and the Roman Catholics] stood over against each other, poised for conflict.[71]

**Focus Verse**: Hold on to the pattern of sound words that you heard from me, in faith and love in Christ Jesus (2 Timothy 1:13).

## Questions for Reflection and Discussion

1. How did the First Diet of Speyer seek to establish unity in the empire?

2. How did those who agreed with Martin Luther come to be called "Protestants"?

3. What prompted the writing of the Augsburg Confession?

Martin Luther's Final Days

# Chapter 12

# Death and Legacy

The Protestant Reformation continued to spread. The Protestant states organized into the League of Schmalkald in order to defend themselves if Emperor Charles V should seek to compel them to return to the religion of the pope. Due to troubles with both the French and the Turkish Empire, Charles V needed the help of the Protestants. So two years after the Augsburg Confession was published, the Peace of Nuremberg–stating that the Protestants could remain in their faith, but could not seek to extend it to other territories, in exchange for which they would support the Emperor against the Turks–was signed in 1532.

Meanwhile, "Luther lived on at Wittenberg, translating, writing, visiting, teaching, and planning for the further advance of the Reformation."[72] Lutheran ministers ignored the Peace of Nuremberg, and they continued to spread Protestant teaching throughout the Holy Roman Empire. These ministers believed their actions to be justified by Acts 4:19-20, in which Peter and John argued that they should obey God rather than people in regard to the gospel proclamation.

"In early January 1546, at the age of sixty-two, Luther returned to the town of his birth, Eisleben."[73] Luther had been summoned to Eisleben in order to resolve a serious dispute between two noblemen concerning the division of some property. Luther answered the summons though he was in extremely poor health. The weather and then the complicated nature of the dispute prevented Luther from returning home for rest and recuperation. The noblemen finally came to a resolution in their dispute, and Luther was preparing to return home to his wife, when he became seriously ill. At 1AM on February 18, 1546, Martin Luther woke from a fitful sleep in severe pain. He repeated in Latin Psalm 31:5, *"In manus tuas commendo spiritum meum, redemisti me, domine Deus veritatis:"* "Into thy hand I commit my spirit; thou hast redeemed me, O Lord God of truth." His friend Justus Jonas, who had been keeping watch over him, asked, "Reverend father, will you die steadfast in Christ, and in the doctrine you have preached?" Luther responded—loud and firm—with a simple, "Yes." He died before the sun rose.

Timothy George notes:

> Luther's body was placed in a tin coffin and returned to Wittenberg where it was laid to rest in the Castle Church on the door of

which Luther had posted the *Ninety-five Theses* nearly thirty years before.[74]

Martin Luther was a pastor, theologian, and university professor. In each of these facets to his vocation, Luther was characterized by his teachings, and these impact Christians across the globe to this day. Among Martin Luther's key teachings, which have had a lasting impact, are: justification by faith alone, the theology of the Cross, the freedom of a Christian, and the bondage of the will.

According to Martin Luther, justification by faith alone—the teaching that we are counted as right in God's sight only on the basis of our trust in Christ, and not due to anything we have done—"was the 'hinge on which all else turns,' the 'issue on which the church stands or falls.' And Luther saw with astonishing clarity its implications for every other Christian teaching or belief."[75] Luther's whole approach to the Christian life may be summed up in his last written words, "We are beggars, that is true." Our own good works cannot buy us any safety or standing before God. We are beggars: needy, vulnerable, totally lacking any resources with which to save ourselves.[76] We must be justified by faith alone, for as sinners we have nothing in ourselves that could possibly contribute to our salvation.

"For Luther the good news of the gospel was that in Jesus Christ God had become a beggar too. God identified with us in our neediness."[77] As Carl Trueman notes: "Luther's whole theology can be quite accurately summed up as one protracted attempt to direct men and women to God in human flesh, Jesus of Nazareth, and Him as crucified."[78] This is Luther's theology of the Cross: that the power of God, which is in one sense hidden during Christ's weakness and suffering, is–in a greater sense–most perfectly revealed through His humiliation and death on behalf of sinners. Furthermore, the theology of the Cross indicates that we meet God through dying to ourselves. Each of the Gospel accounts– Matthew, Mark, Luke, and John–culminates in the death of Christ on the Cross; each Christian life is characterized by daily taking up a cross: dying to self and following Jesus (Luke 9:23). This is why Luther once wrote, "the Cross alone is our theology."[79]

On the basis of Christ's work on the Cross for sinners, the Christian man is truly, fully free: free from sin and free from the impossible burden of attempting to be counted as right in God's sight by means of law-keeping or adherence to ceremonies devised by men. Yet the freedom of the Christian is tempered by the fact that we are to live for God and others in a self-sacrificial manner. In his book *On the Freedom of a Christian* (1520), Luther famously wrote, "A Christian is a perfectly free lord of all, subject to none; a Christian is a perfectly dutiful servant of all, subject to all."[80] This paradoxical statement is explained by the fact that we are made spiritually free through faith in Christ: we are dependent on Him alone for salvation, and therefore no command or opposition from men can affect the welfare of our souls. On the other hand, because we are focused on Christ and not on ourselves, our actions in life should be motivated by a focus on His glory and on loving sinners whom He died to save.

Christ's work on the Cross was absolutely necessary for our salvation because each one of us—due to the fall of Adam and our own evil choices—is naturally sinful to the very core of our being. Our desires do not line up with God's desires; we each want to rebelliously go our own way rather than humbly relying upon God. As Trueman notes: "Luther had come to see how radically sin affected humanity... that it was so all-consuming that nothing short of death could cure it— and that death he found in the death of Christ on the Cross."[81] Luther explained and defended this teaching concerning human sinfulness in his book *The Bondage of the Will* (1525), which he felt to be chief among his written works. As J.I. Packer notes:

> *The Bondage of the Will* is the greatest piece
> of theological writing that ever came from

Luther's pen. This was his own opinion. Writing... on July 9th, 1537, with reference to a complete edition of his works, [Luther] roundly affirmed that none of them deserved preservation save the little children's Catechism and *The Bondage of the Will*; for only they, in their different departments, were 'right' (*justum*).[82]

Luther felt that the doctrine concerning the bondage of the human will to sin was crucial, for it is only when we understand the desperate nature of our situation that we seek the freedom found through the Cross.

More could be said regarding the legacy of Martin Luther. As Roland Bainton noted, "Luther did the work of more than five men" in Bible translation, the setting of liturgy, catechism, preaching, and the writing of hymns.[83] The movement spearheaded by Luther "gave the impetus which sometimes launched and sometimes helped to establish the other varieties of Protestantism [groups of churches that were formed in protest against the Roman Catholic Church]. They all stem in some measure from him." But even the Roman Catholic Church must admit that it owes much to Luther, in that it "received a tremendous shock from the Lutheran Reformation and a terrific urge to reform after its own pattern."[84]

Christians today the world over have struggled with sin, found assurance of salvation in the Cross of Christ alone, and have looked to the Scripture alone as our only infallible, final authority. Many of us—whether knowingly or not—interpret our own experiences based in part on the pattern set by how Martin Luther interpreted his experiences both in struggling with the text of Romans 1:17 and in defending his faith against the power structure of the Roman Catholic Church.

**Focus Verse**: But he said to them all, "If anyone wants to come after me, he must deny himself, and take up his cross daily, and follow me" (Luke 9:23).

## Questions for Reflection and Discussion

1. What did Martin Luther consider to be the "issue on which the church stands or falls"? What did he mean by this term?

2. According to Martin Luther, what were his two greatest writings?

3. What are some ways in which Martin Luther still influences people today?

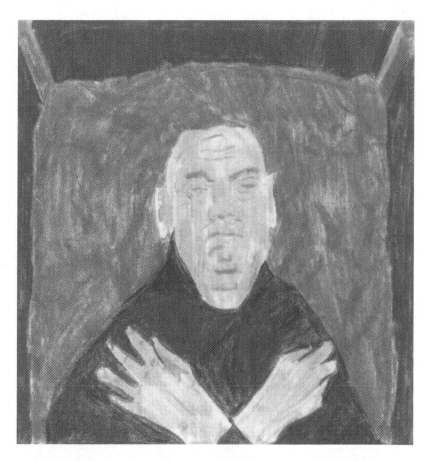

Martin Luther at Rest

# Endnotes

[1]  Roland Bainton, *Here I Stand: A Life of Martin Luther* (Nashville: Abingdon Press, 1978), 18.

[2]  Timothy Lull, *Martin Luther's Basic Theological Writings* (Minneapolis: Augsburg Fortress, 2005), 3-4.

[3]  Virgil Robinson, *Luther the Leader* (Ithaca, MI: A.B. Publishing, 1997), 7-12.

[4]  Justo Gonzales, *The Story of Christianity, Volume 2* (San Francisco: Harper Collins, 1985), 15-16.

[5]  Bainton, 25.

[6]  Robinson, 17-20.

[7]  Gonzales, 16.

[8]  Bainton, 27.

[9]  Robinson, 23.

[10]  Bainton, 34.

[11]  Robinson, 26.

[12]  Ibid., 27.

[13]  Bainton, 30.

[14]  Bainton, 30-32.

[15]  Robinson, 29-38.

[16]  Bainton, 36-38.

[17]  Robinson, 28-29.

[18]  Bainton, 39.

[19]  Ibid., 45-47.

[20]  Lull, 8-9.

[21] Heiko Oberman, *Luther: Man Between God and the Devil* (Yale University Press, 2006), 153.

[22] William Kent, "Indulgences," *The Catholic Encyclopedia*, Vol. 7 (New York: Robert Appleton Company, 1910) Accessed 5 Jun. 2013 <http://www.newadvent.org/cathen/07783a.htm>.

[23] Samuel Macauley Jackson, ed., *The New Schaff-Herzog Encyclopedia of Religious Knowledge* (Grand Rapids: Baker Book House, 1953), 165.

[24] Bainton, 53.

[25] Ibid., 54.

[26] Denis R. Janz, ed., *A Reformation Reader* (Minneapolis: Fortress Press, 2008), 57-59; Mandell Creighton, *A History of the Papacy During the Period of the Reformation*, Vol. 5 (New York: Longmans, Green, and Co., 1894), 64.

[27] Bainton, 59.

[28] Ibid., 60.

[29] Oberman, 188.

[30] Bainton, 60-61.

[31] Heinrich Bornkamm, *Luther's World of Thought* (St. Louis: Concordia Publishing House, 1958), 38.

[32] Bainton, 60-61.

[33] Oberman, 74-75.

[34] Gonzales, 23.

[35] Robinson, 43.

[36] Gonzales, 23-24.

[37] Bainton, 72.

[38] Ibid., 73.

[39] Ibid.

[40] Ibid.

[41] This week-long debate between Eck and Carlstadt shows that this doctrine– known as the doctrine of "depravity"– was central to Protestant Reformational teaching.

[42] Bainton, 89.

[43] Ibid., 90.

[44] Ibid., 105.

[45] A "papal bull" is an official, public decree of the pope containing a specific engraved seal; the lead or gold used to make the seal would first have to be melted down, thus the word "bull," from the Latin *bullire*: "to boil."

[46] Robinson, 60.

[47] Ibid.

[48] Ibid.

[49] Bainton, 141.

[50] Ibid.

[51] That is to say: Luther would appear before the whole group called to the Diet, rather than a relatively small sub-group.

[52] Ibid., 142-143.

[53] Ibid., 143.

[54] Ibid., 143-144.

[55] Ibid., 144.

[56] Bainton, 158.

[57] Robinson, 72; Bainton, 165.

[58] Bainton, 223.

[59] Robinson, 82.

[60] Ibid., 225.

[61] Ibid.

[62] Ibid., 225-226; Philip Schaff, *History of the Christian Church* (Oak Harbor, WA: Logos Research Systems, Inc., 1997), 7.5.77.

[63] Lull, 159-160.

[64] The emperor's brother, Archduke Ferdinand I of Austria, presided over the First Diet of Speyer; the emperor was unable to personally attend due to commitments in other territories.

[65] Robinson, 77.

[66] Gonzales, 43.

[67] Janz, 150.

[68] Gonzales, 43.

[69] Janz, 150.

[70] Gonzales, 43-44.

[71] Bainton, 254.

[72] Robinson, 94.

[73] Timothy George, *Theology of the Reformers* (Nashville: Broadman & Holman Publishers, 1988) 102.

[74] George, 103.

[75] Janz, 77.

[76] George 104.

[77] Ibid.

[78] Carl R. Trueman, *Reformation: Yesterday, Today, and Tomorrow* (Scotland: Christian Focus Publications, 2000), 48.

[79] Martin Luther, *Luther's Commentary on the First Twenty-Two Psalms* (Minneapolis: Lutherans in All Lands Co., 1903), 289.

[80] Lull, 393.

[81] Trueman, 20-21.

[82] J.I. Packer, "Historical and Theological Introduction," Martin Luther, *The Bondage of the Will* (Grand Rapids, MI: Revell, 2002), 40.

[83] "Liturgy" refers to the order of worship in a church service. "Catechism" refers to teaching–usually religious teaching–by means of a series of scripted questions and answers.

[84] Bainton, 301-302.

# Bibliography

Bainton, Roland. Here I Stand: A Life of Martin Luther. Nashville: Abingdon Press, 1978.

Bornkamm, Heinrich. Luther's World of Thought. St. Louis: Concordia Publishing House, 1958.

Creighton, Mandell. A History of the Papacy During the Period of the Reformation, Vol. 5. New York: Longmans, Green, and Co., 1894.

George, Timothy. Theology of the Reformers. Nashville: Broadman & Holman Publishers, 1988.

Gonzales, Justo. The Story of Christianity Volume 2. San Francisco: Harper Collins, 1985.

Jackson, Samuel Macauley, ed. The New Schaff-Herzog Encyclopedia of Religious Knowledge. Grand Rapids: Baker Book House, 1953.

Janz, Denis R., ed. A Reformation Reader. Minneapolis: Fortress Press, 2008.

Kent, William. "Indulgences," The Catholic Encyclopedia, Vol. 7. New York: Robert Appleton Company, 1910.

Lull, Timothy. Martin Luther's Basic Theological Writings. Minneapolis: Augsburg Fortress, 2005.

Luther, Martin. The Bondage of the Will. Grand Rapids, MI: Revell, 2002.

Luther, Martin. Luther's Commentary on the First Twenty-Two Psalms. Minneapolis: Lutherans in All Lands Co., 1903.

Oberman, Heiko. Luther: Man Between God and the Devil. Yale University Press, 2006

Robinson, Virgil. Luther the Leader. Ithaca, MI: A.B. Publishing, 1997.

Schaff, Philip. History of the Christian Church. Oak Harbor, WA: Logos Research Systems, Inc., 1997.

Trueman, Carl R. Reformation: Yesterday, Today, and Tomorrow. Scotland: Christian Focus Publications, 2000.